30 Days of Prayer:

Healing Autoimmunity for Women

Ruschelle Khanna

Edited by Deb Coman and Linda Stubblefield

For More Information go to

www.30daysofprayer.org

For Abby and Amber S.

Table of Contents

Acknowledgements

This book would not be possible without the support of my husband who takes care of me daily. You are my rock and I am so thankful for you.

Many thanks to mom, dad and Toni for always being there and believing in me. I also appreciate you taking care of the dog while I was ill. No, you cannot keep him.

Thank you Mama, Papa, Deepali and Aasheesh for your endless prayers and love. I love you so much.

Thank you Marble Collegiate Church for your Stephen Ministers program which saved my life.

Thank you to all my mothers and fathers at Lane United Methodist Church. Special thank you to Nan for talking me through ideas and properly referencing the Scripture. Thank you Preacher Steve for first teaching me to pray.

I could not have imagined collecting my thoughts in an organized manner during this difficult time without the support of my dear friends, Caryn and Kirsi. You both believed in me and gave me the encouragement to keep writing.

Introduction

By Ruschelle Khanna

What does it mean to be "healed"? In a broad sense, the word means that we are relieved of physical disease. The Bible is full of stories of healing. And while Jesus is considered the ultimate Healer (capable of making ALL aspects of our life perfect and whole), we almost always refer to those accounts as actual physical experiences. Without denying the reality of miraculous healing, I believe some deeper meaning exists in those accounts more than simply the recovery of flesh from disease.

In March 2014, I experienced a debilitating health crisis that, at times, would leave me crippled, blinded, writhing with seizures and delirious in pain. Over the course of a year, I discovered that I had Lyme disease and began the appropriate treatment. Far more important than determining a diagnosis, I came face-to-face with what I believe it truly means to heal. The understanding that absolutely nothing can separate us from God came to me when I woke up to the joyful present moment that is my gift of life. And so, that awareness has been my definition of healing ever since.

It is my hope that in sharing this collection of

prayers, reflections and activities that you, too, can begin to use your physical experience to deepen your relationship with God. My severe, inflammatory pain was an absolute gift that woke me up to the fullness of God. My anguish provided me with a realization that no matter my physical state, I am alive, fully awake and whole. My pain also showed me that I am already fully healed in the most important area of my life, that being my relationship with the Holy Spirit.

During one moment of intense pain, I heard an inner voice that I can only accept as God's saying to me: "I am amazing and amazed." This statement has been my mantra ever since. Every time I am knocked out of the present moment by fear, doubt, anger, jealousy or physical pain, all I have to do is practice coming back to the present, and there He is. I believe that if I live in the present moment, I will remain healed. It is not fully in my hands if my body will ever completely catch up, and I am okay with that reality. I do the best I can, day by day, and vow not to worry about the future. We forget, that no matter what we are experiencing from one moment to the next, in the present moment, we are always perfectly well.

Nothing is more powerful than prayer in cultivating present moment living. No matter the style we choose, be it active prayer through ritual; contemplative meditative listening; reading prayers aloud; or engaging in group prayer; we are all still engaging in the practice of connection to God in the now. This devotional is meant to inspire and enrich your prayer experience through daily readings, reflective questions to answer in a journal on your own, as well as activities to help you reconnect with your body and emotions along your healing journey.

Before We Get Started

The art of healing is an experience in acceptance. This is much more than simply accepting your current circumstances. It requires a rational view of the moment you have before you. This devotional is intended to deepen your alliance with the presence of God, our true source of healing. As you read through Scripture, writings and reflections, you may find disagreement with some writings or ways of experiencing healing. I encourage you to approach the readings with curiosity, noting any sections that raise strong emotions. The following principles are the foundation on which healing can be built. Read through these daily to refocus your intentions on healing.

The Basic Principles of Healing:

1. True healing goes beyond the absence of physical dis-ease. Healing is the ability to continuously practice living in the present

moment, no matter the circumstances, as you approach experiences with curiosity and love.

2. We are defined by love. Our worth is not defined by physical experiences. Our value has already been set by our Creator. We are a priceless, unique expression of God.

3. We are responsible for our healing. Our body is a temple. The body you are currently experiencing is a gift. It allows for the experience of consciousness. It is our responsibility to do everything we can to provide for, nourish and support its optimal function.

4. Healing requires letting go of the negative. Old habits and ways of thinking hinder our ability to heal. Though, perhaps valuable in the past, they can now weigh us down. Healing requires us to make time to let go of hurts and surrender to the healing process.

5. Healing requires acceptance of the positive. We will only heal when we accept it into our lives. If we see ourselves as victims of circumstance, we will always look for someone else to make us whole.

How to Use This Daily Devotional for Your Healing

There are a number of ways to use the material in this book to improve your overall health. This section offers you a guide with some specific ideas about how to get started. This devotional can be used either individually or within a group. In my experience, I have loved using devotionals privately but found a deeper experience when my thoughts and writings were shared with others. No matter which way you choose, committing to improved health and prayer for 30 days is sure to produce positive results in your life.

Set aside a designated time each day to commit to the readings, reflections and prayers. The activities are always optional and can be done in your designated time or scheduled throughout the day. In reading through the material, remember that setting aside time for prayer is a cornerstone in your spiritual practice. I have tried to include many different ways to deepen your prayer experience. While this devotional is meant to serve as a guide, I hope it also sparks your creativity to find new ways to connect with your spiritual journey.

What to Expect

I assume that if you are reading this, you are looking to be healed from a physical condition, likely an autoimmune disorder or disease, but this is a practice that can benefit even the healthiest of bodies. Many of us have worked for a very long time at trying to find what is wrong in our health, searching for help and answers, visiting specialist after specialist with little progress. Sometimes we wish we could return to our "old body" or just have one day without some strange sensation. Often, all we want is for all the signs of illness to just go away.

While there isn't a quick fix or a one-size-fits-all answer, healing is an achievable goal. What is healing to you may look completely different to someone else. Each of us will have a unique experience finding our personal definition of healing. For me, healing was not so much about my physical body being healed (although I still would like my optimal health restored), but more about my spirit being developed in a way that I could handle any obstacle life had in store for me. There were certainly days when I was angry and approached meals, medical visits and other daily tasks with a sense of dread. But the underlying foundation to all of my days recovering was a deep sense that this experience was here for me, rather than happening to me. The farther along I go in my journey, the more I realize it is actually a gift. That said, below are a list of things to expect (and not expect) from this devotional.

You CAN Expect:

- You CAN expect that throughout this next month you will begin to develop a clear understanding of your relationship with illness and your personal definition of healing.

- You CAN expect support and encouragement from the readings, from me and from a community of others sharing in your experience.
- You CAN expect to be challenged. Healing is a journey and no trip is without its share of twists, turns, dives and spins.
- You CAN expect improvement in your prayer life. Committing time and focus to deepening your prayer experience will always result in learning. This devotional is written from my perspective of healing and we are certain to see differently in some aspects. Allowing me to share my experience with you will be one more reference point and guidepost along your journey.

What this devotional is NOT:

- This devotional is NOT a replacement for medical advice. While I suggest certain resources and ideas for healing, you and your physician always make the final call about your healthcare plan.
- This devotional is NOT the final word on your healing. You have the power to make the right decisions related to your health. It is meant to inspire and expand your prayer life as well as your capacity to heal.

What You Will Need:

- Designated time to devote to reading and writing.
- A notebook.
- An open mind.
- A willingness to heal.

Week 1:

Sitting With the Flame

Welcome to week one of 30 Days of Prayer: Healing Autoimmunity for Women. This week begins our exploration of illness and healing as a way to deepen our prayer life. The theme for week one is to begin sitting with our inner flame. Autoimmunity is essentially an inflammation of our nerves and organs. By looking at our body's ability to produce heat (albeit painful at times), we are reminded of God's use of fire to communicate His Word and to cleanse the soul of impurities. In a way, our body, with its immune system working overtime, is communicating valuable information about what it needs as well as cleansing the body of unwanted substances. In this first week, we will begin to focus internally through prayer and contemplation at what it means to listen carefully to both our body and to the Holy Spirit.

DAY 1:

STOP RUNNING FROM YOUR PAIN

"But he was pierced for our transgressions, he was crushed for our iniquities; the punishment that brought us peace was upon him, and by his wounds we are healed." (Isaiah 53:5)

The journey to healing a wounded body can be a long one. Feeling lonely, abandoned and overwhelmed are all familiar states. At times, it can even seem difficult relating to those around us. Most days we long to have our old body back, a new life, or even a brief moment of relief. These thoughts are all simply distractions. God's message is that we be still and stop running from our pain. God urges us to accept our life in its entirety—pain and all. That is not to say that God wants us to suffer. In fact, quite the opposite is true. When we become still with our circumstances, we can fully and deeply recognize the joy of living—no matter the pain.

In beginning this devotional, we will dive into the infinite love of Christ that is available in order to heal. With autoimmunity, so often we tend to look at heat and inflammation as a symptom to be extinguished. But Luke 3:16 gives another connotation to flame: "I baptize you with water, but one who is more powerful than I will come, the straps of whose sandals I am not worthy to untie. He will baptize you with the Holy Spirit and fire. God's love is a healing flame."

The idea that our immune systems have turned on us, i.e., setting fire to our temple, is not particularly helpful in terms of healing. Instead, the notion that our immune system is working as hard as it can to keep us healthy, is more in line with God's beautiful expression of the human body. We have the ability to choose how we see our physical experience. We can choose to identify with an illness or with the divine miracle that we are—perfection in this and every moment.

Prayer

Today, Lord, I take this natural cleansing flame, my immune system, that has been given to me and turn to it as my friend. I notice all the ways that my body is working hard at cleansing me and making me new. I stand firm in the light of Your love, knowing that my body and spirit are eternally alive in You. Amen.

Reflection: Rethinking Autoimmunity

What are some negative thoughts you have had about your body and illness? Write down 3-5 of these negative thoughts. Example: My body is attacking itself.

Take these negative thoughts, one at a time, and turn them into loving statements about your physical experience. Example: My body is working so hard for me in finding new ways to heal and thrive every day.

Action: Setting Up Your Prayer Space

Do you have a space in your home specifically dedicated to prayer and meditation? If so, take today to buy some candles or something special to add to your space. If not, take some time to designate an area in your home to prayer. Here are three simple tips to setting up your space:

1. Include a short, written statement that prompts you to pray. This might be a   favorite Bible verse or inspiring quote.
2. Include all the senses. Include images, tokens from a special occasion, candles and flowers. If possible, set up your space in an area where you can play worship music.
3. Think of your space as living/breathing space, always growing and changing as your needs change. As you move through these next 30 days, be open to adding items and rearranging others in the space you are designating for prayer.

DAY 2:

BE STILL

"He says, "Be still and know that I am God; I will be exalted among the nations, I will be exalted in the earth. "" (Psalm 46:10)

When evening comes and the body is restless, we look everywhere for relief. At times, we feel that we are doing everything possible and still no relief is coming. Then the mind tends to wander, and then we become overtaken by fear. Why can't our bodies simply be still, behave and feel good? And then respite finally happens. Something gives, and relief comes from somewhere. Maybe it's in a good meal or the laugh of our children. We are reminded that behind all of the trembling and agitation, there is a sweet, still "something" that never leaves us.

One of the mind's biggest challenges is to be still. We know the benefits of prayer and meditation, yet the mind still resists. Even while experiencing the middle of a deep, satisfying quietude, the mind nevertheless wants to shout and scream and run to some other comfort. But like a little child who needs gentle prodding, we must regularly return to God's silence for the reminder that this restless body is a vessel ready to blossom.

Prayer

God of silence, I come to You today—not with a request—but simply to listen. I open my heart and mind, welcoming Your stillness to fill me from head to toe. Your silence speaks volumes to my arms, my legs, my torso, my mind. I hear Your stillness with my entire being. Amen.

Reflection: Listening to the Restless Mind

How do you view your restless body and mind? In what ways do you run from it rather than listening deeply?

Activity: Silent Walking Meditation

Today plan to spend time in nature. Turn off the phone. Pay attention to all the sounds, smells and sights around you. Take big breaths. Try to stay focused on walking, letting go of to do lists and other mental distractions. Ten minutes is a great start.

DAY 3:

CULTIVATE PATIENCE

"You have persevered and have endured hardships for my name, and have not grown weary." (Revelation 2:3)

God has not forgotten you. Receiving a diagnosis that most physicians say is a degenerative life sentence is not an easy one to hear. The Christian view of illness is not the perspective of the masses. Your body is an amazing creation, perfectly capable of healing. Not only do we require patience for ourselves but for all those around us who provide care. We even need to cultivate patience for those who don't believe we can heal and for those who don't understand our pain.

Physical healing takes time. The nature of autoimmunity is the response to your body fighting extremely hard to regain balance from whatever it views as foreign. Breathing deeply, eating well, making ourselves a priority, connecting with love and taking part in restorative activities all make up the days and moments of our healing. Enjoy the journey. Jump on the trampoline a bit more, Google cat videos, dance in the living room. Thinking and acting as if you are healed can be very helpful. Just remember there is no pressure here, especially to feel better.

Spiritual healing is our focus. The human condition of birth, illness and death is God's divine vehicle for us to grow closer to our fullest expression. At times, healing is expressed, not in the outward appearance of an improved physical state, but in the remembrance that we are eternal. Think to yourself, "I am healed," regardless of physical circumstances.

Prayer

Dear God, I am thrilled with where I am. Thank You for this life. Thank You for small steps that are meant to be enjoyed. I feel the power or who You are. Through Your power, I will not be discouraged. Today, I slow down, I am patient. I enjoy the place where I am.

Reflection: Forgiving Ourselves

Today, I forgive myself for being impatient. I understand why I feel that way. But ultimately, my body and mind are working so hard to survive. Sometimes I become restless because I know that I am meant to move beyond survival and into thriving. Today, I turn my attention to ways that I am doing exceptionally well. When I think on those things, I give myself some much needed praise.

Activity: Writing About Patience

Consider the following quotes about being patient:

"Patience, persistence and perspiration make an unbeatable combination for success" – Napolean Hill

"Rivers know this: there is no hurry. We shall get there some day." – A.A. Milne, Winnie the Pooh

Now, consider that you are the author of your life story. Now write your own personal quote about patience (or lack thereof).

DAY 4:

KEEP THE FOCUS ON YOU

"A heart at peace gives life to the body, but envy rots the bones." (Proverbs 14:30)

Making comparisons can be one of the most dangerous things that prohibits healing. It can seem as though life goes on for everyone else with no worries, while we sit struggling with decreased functioning and pain. In any relationship, there is no more destructive emotion than jealousy. Entertaining such an emotion erodes any chance of love. Jealousy is tricky. The issue is not one between you and another person; rather, it is to be resolved solely within your heart. When you are happy and confident with your life, all need for jealousy fades away.

The inflammation of autoimmune diseases can knock us off our game for a bit. Regaining mental clarity and finding new ways to function and relate takes a tremendous amount of energy. It can also be a bit of a blow to our confidence. Just think back and remember other times in your life when your confidence took a hit. However, if you recall, your current success was built upon these experiences.

What we need to possess is unwavering confidence. The place to establish this is in living as Christ lived, having confidence in Christ. We need the type of confidence that can heal the sick, rock the establishment and carve a new path for the world! Amazingly, we have access to this with a simple calling out to God.

Prayer

My Creator, some days I feel disconnected from myself and from You. I feel scattered and less than myself. I come to You today sharing an honest pain. This pain can cause me to look around, thinking I am less than perfect. I thank You for connection and organization of thought. In You, I know my memory is strong. My ability to create a joyful life comes easy when I meditate on You.

Reflection: Scripture for Strength

In those moments when I am feeling really bad about my experience, I will reflect on the Scripture that says: "I can do all this through Him who gives me strength." (Philippians 4:13) I have confidence in Christ.

Activity: Writing About Jealousy

Write down some things that you have felt jealousy about since you have been sick. Example: I am jealous of mothers because I can't have children.

Now, as these examples relate to you, rewrite those phrases with love. Example: I rejoice in seeing healthy families around me grow.

DAY 5:

STRENGTHENING FAITH

"Do not be anxious about anything, but in every situation, by prayer and petition, with thanksgiving, present your requests for God." (Philippians 4:6, 7)

Rather than reserving prayer for difficult times, worship or a specific time of day, the Apostle Paul reminds us, beautifully, that prayer is to happen without ceasing. God's presence is available in the sacred and mundane tasks throughout the day. In this way, He has given us mastery over our lives. God wants to be with us as we experience every aspect of life. Often, we pick and choose parts of ourselves that we admire or dislike. Paul encourages us to use all of our experience to strengthen our faith. If something seems difficult, we must take the opportunity to see how God wants us to grow. We are never victims in God's eyes.

Joel Osteen, Pastor of Lakewood Church in Houston, Texas often refers to Christians as "victors," rather than "victims." There is only one way to be a victor, and that is to see our lives as valuable, worthy of all the goodness life has to offer. Victims take the stance that they are not worthy, and are capable of being mistreated, neglected and unwillingly told how to live their lives. Being an advocate for ourselves is one of the most powerful things we can do for self-care. Speaking up brings life into our faith, desires and accomplishments. It is also a powerful way to bring life into our healing process.

Prayer

Today, I am unbound and awake. I pray, speak, and act in ways that call God deeper into every area of my life. I call myself healthy, glorious, and blessed. The power that is in me is God's power. I am well. My eyes see the light that guides my path. My voice speaks words of healing. My feet walk with lightness. My strength is restored.

Reflection: Authentic Listening and Speaking

What are some areas of your life where you have limited God's voice? Are there times when you could have been a better advocate for yourself?

Activity: Acting on Faith

Today, move beyond prayer and take action on one health related goal. Maybe you need to follow up on appointments, do some research or just eat a healthy meal. No matter how small, stop procrastinating and complete a task.

Your body is a glorious gift in all its different seasons. How can you use your body, as it is today to be more present with God? No excuses! Note how you feel after completing the task.

DAY 6:

LOVING YOUR WHOLE EXPERIENCE

"For You created my inmost being; you knit me in my mother's womb. I praise You because I am fearfully and wonderfully made; Your works are beautiful, I know that full well. My frame was not hidden from you when I was made in the secret place, when I was woven together in the depths of the earth." (Psalm 139: 13-15)

The absolute miracle of our body and conscious experience is something that we take completely for granted most of the time. If we fully grasped how wonderfully made we were, the adoration for our bodies would simply pour out of us, daily. When we look at our bodies as sick, weak, and incapable, we are denying the holy experience that is right in front of us.

Do you ever use harsh words to refer to your body or your illness? Are there parts of you that you would rather cut off or get rid of? Healing is a perfect time to take a deeper look at the parts of ourselves we might otherwise ignore or wish to change. It is a human desire to want to be better. But improvement starts with loving and acknowledging where we are today. Every function that your body has, serves to keep you well. Every feature you were given was perfectly placed.

34

Being critical of our body's limitations does not serve us in healing. Sometimes our self-talk can run wild. Rather than spending time wishing you were different, stronger, leaner or healthier, claim it now. We can say to ourselves: "My body is perfect for me in this life. It serves all my needs. I am perfectly made."

Prayer

God, the One Who formed me perfectly in Your image, I thank You for my shape and form. I am overwhelmed and amazed at the body that daily carries me throughout this world for no other reason than to experience joy. I praise Your name. My being is something of wonder—full of life and love and thanksgiving. Amen.

Reflection: Looking At Our Bodies With Love

Do parts of your body displease you? If so, is there another way to look at your body that is loving?

Activity: The Body Scan

Take 3 to 5 minutes to sit quietly and find your breath. As you breathe, begin with the top of your head and slowly scan down your body, from head to toe. With each breath, check in with each body part. Ask them how they are doing. Thank them for working so hard. Make notes about your experience when you are finished.

DAY 7:

LIMITLESS LOVE

"I have been crucified with Christ and I no longer live, but Christ lives in me. The life I now live in the body, I live by faith in the Son of God, who loved me and gave himself for me." (Galatians 2:20)

This week has focused on sitting with a number of different types of pain and discomfort. We have explored the idea that through what seems like suffering, we have the capacity to sit a bit closer to the flame of God. Experiencing autoimmunity allows for a particular practice in patience, perseverance, understanding, and focus. The physical sensations are often secondary to our mental and spiritual battles. Establishing stillness, being patient and staying focused on our healing, are challenges that have the potential to lead to a deep and unwavering faith.

By sitting still, we learn that we are perfectly and divinely made anew in every moment. Prayer and contemplation affirm that our past cannot overshadow the blessing to which we look forward in this new and present moment. And this affirmation is only accomplished by respecting and appreciating the body we are given in this very moment. We must accept that we are whole in this moment in time.

Once we choose to accept wholeness, only one thing can follow—limitless self-love. Imagine the love that Christ has for us. Striving to have that type of love for ourselves leads to the confidence in Christ that is needed to navigate anything: medical visits, relationship issues, financial struggles and whatever life can send in our direction.

Prayer

Limitless Creator, I am inspired daily by Your unbounded love. I acknowledge that through Your love, I no longer live for selfish reasons but for a love that connects me to everyone and everything. I acknowledge that I am whole and perfect in Your sight. I will approach this day with Christ-like confidence, respect, appreciation and grace.

Reflection: Embodying Christ

How would your life change if you daily practiced Christ-like confidence? What opportunities and new relationships might be made by this type of living?

Activity: Confidence Practice

A recent TED talk by Amy Cuddy describes how our

body language shapes who we are. Cuddy states that two physiological qualities are noticeable in powerful people: higher levels of testosterone (an aggressive hormone) and lower levels of cortisol (a stress hormone).

She states that in only two minutes of practicing what she calls "posturing," we can dramatically change our physiology to that of a person with increased confidence.

Find a private place, preferably with a mirror and begin to make your body and facial expressions as big as possible. For example. Raise your arms out wide and above your head, pull back your shoulders, make your eyes wide and open your mouth. Play around with different variations of this "bigness" for two minutes. Note how you feel before and after.

WEEK 2:

TURN IT OVER

Welcome to week two. In week one, a foundation of contemplative prayer was built to serve as a foundation for your prayer life. This week will address exploring the various ways we can turn things over to God. We will work to expand our vision of what we believe God can handle in our daily lives. Again, we will look at how our current physical experience can be used to open our spirits more fully to all of the good things God has in store for us. We will take a look at both the physical and emotional matters that bind us to our current negative ways of thinking of ourselves and our current condition. This week you will be guided through reflections that challenge your current definition of healing. Finally, you will learn tools to release tension stored in the body, allowing prayer to flow more easily.

DAY 8:

LETTING GO OF THE THINGS THAT BIND US

"Continue to remember those in prison as if you were together with them in prison, and those who are mistreated as if you yourselves were suffering."
(Hebrews 13:3)

Illness brings the illusion of restriction through both physical and cognitive limitations. Sometimes these restrictions are opportunities to be patient with ourselves and to listen carefully to the signals our bodies are giving us. Illness is really an opportunity to be attentive, to nurture and to care for ourselves in a way that we might not, if we were otherwise healthy.

Today's Scripture speaks to the needs of prisoners and their mistreatment. There may be times when we feel like a prisoner in our own body. How often do you see "healthy" people taking their bodies and abilities for granted? The world may seem to be moving right along without our even being able to get out of bed. This is the real struggle: realizing that our current moment is precious—whether viewed from the bed or the bustle of life. When we are feeling bad, that is one difficult concept to understand. Patiently, in the moment, we simply do what we can. We all have days when no task seems to be completed, or we are restricted by pain. On those days, simply do one thing. Continue to move forward. Movement is life. If you are moving forward (even a little bit), you are not restricted. You are free. Sometimes the vibrant movement we have is in our prayers.

Prayer

God I know that you accept me and all my emotions. I know that you are big enough to handle my frustration, anger, and disappointments. You provided me a range of emotions to experience rather than suppress. My emotions are another reminder of the infinite ways I have available to experience You. Today, I will honor my emotions, listening carefully to what they are saying and responding with love.

Reflection: Addressing Our Anger

The writer of the book of Hebrews penned the opening Scripture for those free Christians to remember the people who were unjustly placed in prison. Did you ever feel angry that you became ill "unjustly" or without reason? Similar to a wrongly accused prisoner, we might become angry at our current circumstances. We really didn't do anything "wrong" to deserve this restriction. It can be infuriating. The only thing that matters is what we do with our anger.

Activity: Pray for Others

Today, spend some time in prayer for someone who you believe is suffering more, or in more bondage, than you are. If you have the chance, reach out to that person. Connect and tell him you are thinking of him and that he is loved.

Remember to make note of anything that comes up today as you go through prayer, reflection and action.

DAY 9:

MOVING FROM FATIGUE TO VITALITY

"Do you not know? Have you not heard? The Lord is the everlasting God, the Creator of the ends of the earth. He will not grow tired or weary, and his understanding no one can fathom."(Isaiah 40:28)

The prophet Elijah is commonly known for his fierce determination, as well as his ability to perform miracles and part waters. He had the vision and connection to overcome anything put in his path. But all of Elijah's days were not productive moments of powerful communication with God. Even Elijah had fearfully depressed days when nothing seemed to be going well. Elijah's crisis is told through 1 Kings 19:1-18. In this passage, we see a side of Elijah that is exhausted, frustrated and negative.

One of the first mistakes often made when we aren't feeling 100 percent is to start comparing ourselves to others. The story of Elijah reminds us of the need to address this wrong thinking in two ways. First, if someone as determined and focused as Elijah can have a bad day, we might not be so harsh on ourselves the next time it happens in our life. Second, Elijah himself fell into the trap of comparing himself to others. The important thing is to catch your blaming thoughts and bring the focus back to your wellbeing.

We are all capable of having more energy. The basis of this belief is found in our willingness to take care of our physical bodies as best as we can. Vitality comes from making good nutritional choices, having proper sleep, doing what we love, watching inspiring things, being uplifted by our community, exercising physically, and prayer. During Elijah's crisis, God told Elijah to rest and eat (1 Kings 19:5-8). Today, following God's simple advice to Elijah still remains a good place to start when we feel fatigued and depressed.

In 1 Kings 19:10 and 11, Elijah begins to dialogue with God, simply telling Him all his frustrations. Taking the time to express your frustration and trapped feelings allows for energy to begin to move in your life. Whether you write down, pray aloud or call a willing friend, expressing your frustrations can give you the needed boost to lift up out of physical depression and fatigue. However, I believe there is more to living than simply being free of fatigue. We should desire to live a life of vitality. When Elijah was at his best, he was advocating for God, as well as using his gifts and talents to the best of his ability. He had found his life's purpose and tried to live up to that standard every day.

Prayer

I am aware that my energy is sent from the universal Spirit, Maker of everything. I am continuously restored and renewed. I know exactly how to improve my condition in any given moment. Whenever I feel weak, tired and unable to go on, I quickly focus my vision on the Light of Life Who replenishes my soul. I accept freedom from fatigue and exchange sluggishness for the excitement of being made anew. Today, I inhale vitality and exhale fatigue.

Reflection: Recalling Enthusiasm

Read 1 Kings 19:1-18. What has been the most energizing aspect of your life? How do you share your enthusiasm for life with others?

Activity: Energy Inventory

- Write the life categories below:
- Prayer Life
- Self-talk
- Nutrition/Food
- Sleep
- Physical Exercise
- Family Relationships
- Worship Community
- Social Relationships

- Media (television, music choices, smart phone)
- Work
- Creativity
- Physical Environment (home, nature, city life)

"Rate each category based on one of the following:"

- Energy Draining
- Neutral
- Somewhat Uplifting
- Fully Energizing

Once you have rated each category, think about making more time for the "Fully Energizing" activities.

DAY 10:

PRACTICING THE SWEET BREATH OF SPIRIT

"The Spirit of God has made me; the breath of the Almighty gives me life." (Job 33:4)

We are healed through our breath. The fundamental filtering organ of the human immune system is our lungs. Unlike our blood, the immune system does not have a 24-hour pump such as the heart to keep it moving. Instead, the immune system relies on the lungs and our breath to pump the lymph fluid throughout our body, fighting infection and healing organs. The breath is our best healing tool. This is why nothing feels better than a big full breath of air. Yet many of us struggle with restricted breathing and feelings of "air hunger." Working to take in one full breath can feel like an all-day task. In searching for a good breath, the rest of our body holds tension and anxiety, causing a chain reaction of restricted muscles all over.

The act of prayer is a perfect time to come back to the breath. We can actually use our prayer time to reconnect quietly to all of the spaces that need to be filled. We have a path, and that path leads to freedom and happiness. Our path is open and expansive. My friend, stop cutting yourself off to be fully present. No matter our condition, the breath is something we can work to improve—even if only a little bit. Abide sweetly in the breath of God.

As long as we have breath, we are called to praise the Lord. Psalm 150:6 states: "Let everything that has breath praise the Lord! Praise the Lord."

Prayer

Holy Breath of Life, God Who gives and sustains life, cleanse my body and heart with every fresh, new breath I take. My lungs are healthy and strong. They easily sustain me. With my inhale, I feel Your love. With my exhale, anxiety and tension are diminished. Today I am made new and filled with love.

Reflection: Focus on Praiseworthy Aspects of Life

How can we keep from praising the Lord if we have breath in our lungs? As you read this, something has to be praiseworthy in your vision. What are those things you see today that can invigorate your desire to connect with life?

Activity: Breathing for Pain Relief

Breathing is one of many chronic pain control

techniques.   Sit quietly and just take four deep breaths in, hold four counts, then exhale four counts.

Gently massage your shoulders, arms and legs.

Repeat 5 breath cycles.

DAY 11:

HONORING SLEEP

"In peace I will lie down in sleep, for you alone Lord make me dwell in safety." (Psalm 4:8)

Sleep is essential to our health and wellbeing. Many wonderful things happen when we sleep, including the organization and storage of information into our long-term memory, restoration of cells and wound healing, and increased clearance of waste products from the brain. People who are sleep deprived do not heal as well those who are well-rested. In fact, your immune system is directly impacted by sleep deprivation. Many studies show a decrease in the white blood cell counts of those who are sleep-deprived. Any healing and self-care routine should include a strong plan to enhance the ease and quality of your sleep.

Although some physical factors such as disruptions in hormones, certain medications and sleep apnea can impact our ability to sleep, there are just as many avenues within our control that can make sleeping much easier. Simple daily routines such as turning off electronics at night; making a comfortable bedroom; taking time for meditation, prayer and deep breathing before bed, as well as non-addictive sleep supplements are all options for improving sleep. Not everything will work for everyone, and it may take several months before a healthy sleep pattern can be established, but with determination and focus, you can restore your sleep quality.

Sleep provides the ability to connect with God on deeper levels including through dreams and through days of increased energy. Neglecting sleep is not an option when aspiring for a healthy, joy-filled life. Although, many dreams we don't remember, some are enjoyable and others not so pleasant, but at other times, dreams can serve as warnings or strong reminders that we need to change things in our life.

Prayer

God of opposites, Creator of sleeping and waking, thank You for the natural balance of day and night. I am amazed at my body's ability to flow naturally with the rhythms of the physical world. I am reminded of Ecclesiastes 3 that states: "There is a time for everything and a season for every activity under heaven." Today, I do my best to honor the natural balance of my days. Every night before going to bed I affirm: I sleep in peace and wake in joy.

Reflection: Committed to Healing

Have you committed to making sleep a sacred time of renewal and healing? Have you placed work or other priorities above your sleep?

Activity: Tune Up Your Sleep

Take time today to evaluate your sleep routine. Choose three to five small changes you could make to improve sleeping. Some of these might include:

- Limit electronic use two hours before bedtime.
- Designate the bedroom as a place for sleeping and being intimate only. This rule means no work, no electronics, no food, etc.
- Develop nighttime rituals including caffeine-free teas, meditation, foot soaks, self-massage, etc.
- Spend time in self-talk before bed, telling your mind "It is time to sleep. You will rest deeply and wake up feeling refreshed."
- Limit eating foods at least two hours before bedtime.
- Limit caffeine use throughout the day.

DAY 12:

ENVISONING YOUR SUPPLE BODY

"From him the whole body, joined and held together by every supporting ligament, grows and builds itself up in love, as each part does its work." (Ephesians 4:16)

The body of Christ has been referred to in Ephesians as a symbol of unity and maturity for the church. Like Christ's body, yours is a sacred tool used to connect with others. Without question, you have the perfect body for your life. Envisioning your body as a perfect creation can come with obstacles—especially when it is full of sore spots, achy joints and pieces that simply do not seem to work very well together. These seeming imperfections or symptoms of disease can lead to our being overly critical, as well as speaking and thinking harshly of ourselves. But adopting God's view of us leaves no room for bullying or self-criticism. There is only room for love. Just as the Ephesians were called to have a unified, loving, mature church with Christ's body as the analogy, we are also called to have a unified, loving mind when thinking about our physical body.

Staying mentally focused on a supple body is more than a good sounding idea. Several research studies show an improvement in muscle tone simply by mentally rehearsing exercises. This is powerful stuff! Matthew 6:22 says: "The eye is the lamp of the body. So, if your eye is healthy, your whole body will be full of light." This verse reminds us that what is in our vision is what becomes true in our reality. Today is the day for each of us to let go of rigid, negative thoughts about our body. It is working so hard for us and deserves lots of positive and reassuring statements that it is performing at its very best.

Prayer

Oh God of movement and grace, today is a new day ripe with the sweetness of life. Let my focus be clear when I look upon myself in the mirror. Let me see clearly the reflection of You that shines out in the world. As my critical thinking diminishes, my body, with all its seeming imperfections, becomes mobile, fluid and free. Today, my lungs are filled with the breath of divine presence, my muscles the strength of Your foundation, my joints the fluidity of life everlasting.

Reflection: Making the body a channel for love

Your supple body is a channel for God's love. From outward appearances, we may have days when we appear or feel rigid, achy and unstable. However, as long as we are going in the direction of a free-flowing mental attitude, the body must follow.

Activity: Visualizing Anesthesia

Aside from deep breathing, another chronic pain relief technique involves visualization of being given an injection of anesthetic into the painful area. This type of visualization can be combined with self massage, heat or ice applied to the painful area.

DAY 13:

BEING LED BY FAITH

"Do not be conformed to this world, but be transformed by the renewal of your mind, that by testing you may discern what is the will of God, what is good and acceptable and perfect." (Romans 12:2)

In healing, as in other aspects of our life, we are led by faith. But faith cannot operate without confidence. Sometimes we must make decisions when we do not have all of the information. The times we go out on a limb to trust people and situations also requires the ability to accept setbacks that, inevitably, will come. In order to be confident, we have to strip away the emotional burdens we carry. We all have our own unique way of lugging around unnecessary relationships, emotions and ways of thinking.

One common weak spot is the neck and shoulders. Not only does our neck have the responsibility of supporting our head (which typically weighs about 10 pounds), but it must follow our vision via information from the optic nerves. This delicate wiring of seeing and responding via the cranial and neck muscles really is quite amazing. To add to that tremendous responsibility, our becoming stressed tends to tighten and overexert these muscles, leaving them immobile and in pain.

The process of eliminating unwanted stress from our upper body is twofold. There is the daily task of both mentally and physically rolling out the tension that immobilizes us. This process is essential because our neck helps us determine which way to go. Without neck and shoulder mobility, we become incapable of clearly determining direction. In essence, our neck mobility is a metaphor for our ability to make good decisions.

Prayer

Holy Spirit, You are the One Who leads me. Whenever I feel stuck or overwhelmed, all I have to do is find stillness, and in that stillness, I find You. You guide me in so many ways. I am most amazed at the way You speak to me through my physical body. In noticing my posture and breath, my body in all its wisdom tells me exactly what it needs. Today, I declare I am right where I am supposed to be. With this perfect body, I have the confidence to move forward toward a better version of me. Amen.

Reflection: How the Body Carries Emotion

What do you think of the expressions "He's a pain in the neck," and "I just can't shoulder this responsibility right now"? Are these expressions you use? Is this a sensitive area for you? In what ways can you start to unload some of those burdens and allow God to help you carry the weight?

Activity: Release Tension in the Neck

Do one or all of the following:

- Sing, chant or hum as long as your heart desires
- Do gentle neck rolls while breathing deeply
- Shrug and roll your shoulders, sitting up nice and tall
- Move your head in a figure 8 motion
- Look up "singing drills for beginners" on Youtube.

DAY 14:

DISCOVERING THE LIGHT TO OUR PATH

"Your word is a lamp to my feet and a light to my path." (Psalm 119:105)

Did you ever have the experience of being lost while on vacation? What a glorious feeling to finally figure out the map, get on the right road and be on your way! Knowing where you are going is a really incredible feeling that eludes most of us throughout our lives. Not feeling our best can present us with a number of things that kick us off our path and send us down dark, uncharted territory. The experience of uncertainty is often a whirlwind of emotions ranging from excitement to fear.

Fear attempts to trick us into believing we have been abandoned. Fear can either be rational or imaginary. Rational fear is based in a genuine need to take action, like making that phone call to a doctor or taking steps to get back on track with your health. Irrational fear immobilizes, shuts us down or makes us hide from our responsibilities. It is important that we practice taking an honest look at what we fear. When we look deeply at our present moment—the only moment we ever have—we realize fear is not an enemy but a signal for examination and change. The practice is to stop looking at situations of pain as "bad" and moments of joy as "good." Instead, look lovingly at all situations with the confidence that God is directing your path through all conditions.

We are called to get up and walk both figuratively and actually. Limitations in mobility can be mentally paralyzing. Not knowing how to navigate physically can cloud our abilities in other areas of our lives, including work and relationships. But we are ever-changing, ever-growing creations not meant to stay the same. The way we related to people when we were children is not the way we relate to people as adults. Literally, every day of our life we must wake up to a new body that must navigate the world in different ways than previously used. Regardless of those changes, we are called to show up, rise to the occasion and do our very best each day.

Prayer

Almighty God, You are the Light of my path. Today, I feel alive in my body from head to toe. The journey of my life is so much fun. I am always led to interesting, fresh and new endeavors. I may have to step through some puddles or drag my legs through mud, but with every step I will enjoy where I am, knowing that You are always with me.

Reflection: Examining Reactions to Fear

How do you generally react to feelings of fear? Do you tend to run or fight? When have feelings of fear served as motivation to make changes?

Activity: List Your Fears

Make a list of your fears divided into two categories: real and irrational. Under each column, list some fears you have about your health. Review the list.

Can you take action to address any of your real fears? How can you begin to think differently about the irrational ones?

WEEK 3:

FEELING GOD IN ALL THINGS

There is not a single aspect of our life, waking or sleeping, of which God is not a part. In week three we will begin to explore the many ways our bodily experiences can enhance our relationship with God. We will learn to view physical sensations as information that fuels our prayer life. Beginning with our figurative inner fire, digestion, we begin to look at our relationship with food as a metaphor for the nourished soul. We will also examine sight as a way to pray for flawed ways of viewing situations. Day 20 will finish the week with a meditation on experiencing more grace in our life.

DAY 15:

LET YOUR FOOD HEAL YOU

"'...And to all the beasts of the earth and all the birds in the sky and all the creatures that move along the ground—everything that has the breath of life in it—I give every green plant for food.' And it was so."
(Genesis 1:30)

Nutrition is the foundation of our health and healing. One of the first things that affects our eating habits is how conscious we are in purchasing, preparing and consuming our food. One term for this process is conscious eating. As children, we can only eat what is prepared for us. Sometimes the choices made by our parents were not always the most nutritious. But as adults, we have almost total control over what, how, and when we eat. Getting into a rhythm with an appropriate nutritional routine takes time, preparation and consistency.

We need support to maintain healthy eating habits. Food is one of those aspects of life that really binds us to others, socially. When health conditions restrict our ability to share in traditional meals with loved ones, we can feel resentful and left out. Having multiple levels of support makes the process of sticking to a healing diet much more manageable.

Making mealtime a sacred experience is one of the most important ways you can help your healing. This practice elevates the way we view food because God is involved in the details of our nutrition. When we start to examine where our food came from, the manner in which it was prepared and even our thought patterns as we are eating, every meal becomes a connection with the Divine One.

Prayer

God Who nourishes me, You provide abundantly for my healing and progress. I know that in this vast world, so many creatures took part in providing my meals. The energy that grew the plants, picked the fruits, fed the animals, transported and prepared my meals is the same energy that pulses through me. When I prepare my meals, You are with me. I will take time to bless my meals, remembering that they are meant for my good.

Reflection: How Is My Nutrition-Related Support System?

What type of support system do you have in place to make sure your nutritional requirements are being met? Are your living environment and family helpful to your dietary needs?

Activity: Tune Up Your Nutrition

Take some time today to reassess your eating habits. Answer the following questions and take one step to improve one of them today based on your answers:

- How can you make your nutritional and eating habits a bit better?
- Do you need more information about eating well for healing autoimmunity?
- Do you have a system for preparing meals in bulk?
- Do you need to schedule time to speak with a professional?

DAY 16:

DIFFERENT WAYS OF SEEING

"Do not be wise in your own eyes; fear the Lord and shun evil." (Proverbs 3:7)

Cranial nerves connect directly to the brain. The optic nerves, which are connected to our eyes, are the only ones considered to be a part of our central nervous system. These nerves are responsible for our perception of depth, clearness of vision and brightness. Optic nerves transmit visual information through the retina directly to the brain. Inflammation of the central nervous system can damage this delicate pathway causing visual limitations. Visiting the eye doctor regularly is crucial for maintaining health when living with autoimmunity.

But seeing is not simply about our physical vision. As Christians, we are called to see the world through the lens of love. Blurry spots of fear can overtake our perception in ways that are far more damaging than being physically blind. There will inevitably be times when it is hard to sift through fear. Some days may come with setbacks and stagnant moments where there seems to be no progress in healing. But the fact that you are reading this page speaks volumes about your focus. As long as you are viewing your life experience from love rather than fear, you have not lost vision. You are not blindly navigating the world. Just as God guides our feet, if we will allow Him, He will use our eyes to see the love in every situation.

Focusing on love is a simple message, but trying to do so for even ten minutes can be much more difficult than it sounds. However, we can do so many things to keep us focused and on track. Daily inspirational reading and podcasts are so helpful. The images and words we choose to keep in our home can be either beneficial or distracting. Also, choosing the types of media we view on a daily basis is so important. Life is difficult enough. It is important that what we choose to put before us is positive and uplifting.

Prayer

Holy God, I praise You for the glorious gift of sight. Wow! Today, I stand amazed looking in the mirror at this wonderful creation. You have made me perfect and whole. When I become discouraged, I will remember that all I have to do is correct my vision. I will reach for love where there is fear. Even if my steps aren't perfect, I will move in the direction of love, remembering that there are many ways to see a situation. I choose to see through Your eyes.

Reflection: Viewing Life With Love

What are your emotional circumstances today? How can you view your current experience with a bit more love?

Activity: Seeing Exercise

Take a minute to sit comfortably wherever you are. Close your eyes, thinking that when you open your eyes, you will scan the room for only the color blue. Next, open your eyes. Notice what your vision focuses on. Close your eyes and decide that when you open them, you will scan the room for only the color red. Open your eyes and scan the room, focusing only on red objects.

This simple example demonstrates how important it is to focus our vision on the things we want to see. Now, each day before you leave the house, vow to focus your vision on something you want to see. Maybe you want a day full of healing or a day full of love. As long as you decide to focus your vision, those circumstances will come to you!

DAY 17:

ENJOYING THE FIRE

"He makes his messengers winds, his ministers a flaming fire." (Psalm 104:4)

Sometimes God whispers, and other times he screams. Physical pain is one of those messages that most would probably place in the "scream" category. Saying that one can experience neurological and muscular pain in a quiet, peaceful way simply isn't realistic. The list of sensations and experiences the nervous system can come up with to alert us of internal danger is unbelievably vast. Words like "overwhelming" and "indescribable" never convey to friends and family what it is actually like to be burning up from the inside. As painful as those moments are, and as bad as we just want them to go away, we must remember that our pain is present to propel us, to move and shake us, to cause us to grow.

Some pain-filled moments are flooded with sadness and intense rage and others are filled with so many emotions we can't even distinguish the feelings. Often, finding the breath and remembering that the pain is temporary are the best solutions we have. In the moment we cry out to God, wondering where He is and why we have been left alone in the mess. But time and again, when coming out of the pain, we see that God never leaves us. He is simply a bit harder to see at times.

Perception of pain plays a major role in how we live our life. Psalm 104 is a beautiful poem displaying God's direction over all of nature. As reflections of God, we, too, have control over so many aspects of our life, especially the painful spots. This ultimate control comes from our perception. Through focusing our minds on the glory of God, life suddenly becomes magical. No aspect of our life is left unaccounted for, particularly moments of physical suffering. Pain can be reframed as a strong motivator for us to continue to live a healthy lifestyle. It can be the push we need to be more present with our families or to finish those projects we have been delaying. Sometimes pain can be so debilitating that our good days are reason for complete and unbridled celebration.

Prayer

Loving God, You know exactly what I need in every moment. My lack of vision keeps me from seeing You in every moment, especially those that are painful. Give me the breath and calmness of mind to search my heart and listen for You. Today, I will remember You especially in my moments of discomfort and pain. I will rejoice in the experience of being alive.

Reflection: Reframing

How can you reframe your experience of pain to work for you? What are your thoughts on the following phrase: "I own my pain. It is mine, and I can do with it as I please."?

Activity: Write a Letter to Your Pain

Let's pretend your pain is a person. Write a quick letter to your pain. Say whatever you would like. Be real and honest. Say exactly what you feel. Make note of your feelings and thoughts after writing your letter.

DAY 18:

HEARING GOD'S CALL

"Here I am! I stand at the door and knock. If anyone hears my voice and opens the door, I will come in and eat with that person, and they with me." (Revelation 3:20)

When Mother Teresa was asked how she prayed to God, her response was "I don't talk. I simply listen." And when asked what God would say, she replied "He listens." The traditional view of prayer in which we ask for things and wait to receive them is only a small portion of the prayer experience. Some would argue that the act of asking for things from God is not only irrelevant but harmful. From a more neutral perspective, asking God for worldly things like health and financial success have a time and place but certainly do not encompass all the ways we can connect with Divinity. What Mother Teresa was describing was the basis of prayer, which is silence. The practice of listening intently to God in a way that brings us more fully into the present moment is a type of prayer that supersedes any worldly desires for improved quality of life we could ever fathom.

Essentially, practicing deep listening with God reminds us that we are alive in the NOW and that in this NOW place, we never have any wants or needs. It reminds us that, in the moment we are sitting in our bedroom or at our desk at work, we are perfectly well. In silent prayer, we can stop searching for something better or feeling as if we aren't enough. All that disappears when we really learn to listen to God's call. That is all He is ever saying. Matthew 6:26 says, "Look at the birds of the air: they neither sow nor reap nor gather into barns, and yet your heavenly Father feeds them. Are you not of more value than they?" This passage reminds us our earthly needs have been cared for. Really, all we have to focus on is opening up to the present moment where God always lives.

Prayer

God, today I call upon You through silence. I wait for You in the still moments and lulls of my day. There I know You are always with me, and I am fulfilled. My heart is full. May I recognize now and throughout the day that I am whole from moment to moment. In this life of wanting, which is conditioned into me, I connect with my wholeness. I understand it is human to always want things different or better. I also understand that because of my present connection with You, I can transcend mental wanting, see it for what it is and live fulfilled.

Reflection: Recalling Stillness

Think of a time have you experienced the presence of God through stillness. What were the physical sensations you remember from this experience?

Activity: Stillness Meditation

Try the silent meditation below. You can set your timer starting at 5 minutes, working up to 20-30 minutes.

By closing down the portion of our minds dedicated to speech—even if we are still engaged in internal dialog—our minds are more free, and we are better able to tune into ourselves. Silent Meditation is the most basic of practices—though to be successful, it requires advanced concentration skills which may take some time to develop. In essence, we sit in a quiet environment, and, clearing our minds of all thoughts, focus on the breath entering and leaving our bodies. When we feel our minds drift, we simply bring them back to our breath. Practiced consistently, this meditation helps us stay present in daily life. - Trungram Gyaltrul Rinpoche

DAY 19:

TURNING OUR TREMBLING INTO PRAYER

"So I prophesied as I was commanded: and as I prophesied, there was a noise, and behold a shaking, and the bones came together, bone to his bone." (Ezekiel 37:7)

There are different types of tremors and tremblings from a mild, jittery feeling to internal continuous tremors. Physiologically, the body trembles when there is an increase in the hormone adrenaline. In fact, in the wild, animals induce trembling in order to release excess energy. Tremors can also occur when excess stresses are placed on the central nervous system like inflammation, infection or a loss of communication between nerves and muscles. We can learn many things through experiencing the sensation of tremors. Maybe our body is warning us to slow down or asking us to practice being still. Like our animal friends, at other times the body may be asking for movement to release trapped and excess energy. In either case, begin to approach every physical sensation with curiosity and love. For a while, let's release the urge to demand our body to be still or to act differently than it can in these moments.

Sensations like anxiety and trembling can make us

feel out of control and angry. It's okay to have anger and frustration over circumstances as long as we don't get stuck there. God is certainly big enough to handle all of our emotions. In fact, every emotion, including the negative ones, can be a huge catalyst for growth. As long as we do not turn our anger inward in the form of shame and self-doubt, we can continue to express how we feel in the moment and move forward. Turn your so-called limitations around.

The opening Scripture passage is taken from Ezekiel 37, which records the story of "The Valley of the Dry Bones." In this prophetic vision, God speaks to Ezekiel of a resurrection of Israel from their having lost hope. Ezekiel sees a pile of bones begin to shake and tremble, but they are not alive. Then just as God breathed life into Adam, He breathed life into the bones (a symbol of the people of Israel). This vision can serve as our prayer reminder that every time we become distracted by, or bring awareness to, our trembling or anxiety, we can recount Ezekiel's vision of the valley of the dry bones and remember that God is breathing new life and hope into every part of our body. After all, spiritually healing is all about how we relate to our experiences.

Prayer

Creator God, You breathed life into my bones. With every inhale and exhale I am reminded that it is the Spirit that allows me to rise up, take control of my life and be healed. Creator God, You strengthen me and sustain me through my trembling and my calm. You allow me to witness the fullness of this human experience with curiosity rather than fear. Using my breath, I listen to my trembling. With every exhale I am soothed.

Reflection: Facing Fear

Have you ever experienced trembling from fear or medical issues? When you begin to experience anxiety or trembling, what types of things do you tell yourself? How might God be using trembling to tell you something?

Activity: Free-writing Through Anger

Begin writing any frustrated or angry thoughts. Set the timer for ten minutes. Without worrying about punctuation or grammar, just begin freely writing. No need to read it again. Don't look at it right away. You can set it aside for review later or immediately throw it away.

DAY 20:

WALKING WITH GRACE

"How beautiful your sandaled feet, O prince's daughter! Your graceful legs are like jewels, the work of an artist's hands." (Song of Songs 7:1)

According to the Oxford Pocket Dictionary, the noun grace has two definitions:

1. simple elegance or refinement of movement.

2. (in Christian belief) the free and unmerited favor of God, as manifested in the salvation of sinners and the bestowal of blessings.

How can we possibly expect to receive God's grace without first internalizing the physical feelings associated with His grace? The mind has such a sneaky way of pushing us out of the glory of our own life. Too often we determine that we aren't worthy of this thing or that thing. We say that we couldn't possibly achieve certain goals or aren't good enough to be around certain types of people. We must begin the practice of calling ourselves worthy and identifying first as the elegant, refined, perfectly designed women that we are.

Some movement practices like yoga teach us that

our body is never the same as it was the day before and that we should approach movement with respect for our present condition. Never assume that your body should perform as it did in the past. Simply put, it is just not yesterday's body but a different one. Letting go of the expectation that the body must perform a certain way allows for us to connect with it in a fresh, nonjudgmental way.

One way to foster our sense of worthiness is to view our body as being full of grace. There are many ways to practice feeling graceful and light. Gentle dancing, yoga or tai chi are great exercises that have been proven to reduce inflammation and boost the immune response. Also, if we were at one time more physically active than we are presently, we can use visualization to recall memories of how our body felt at that time. For most of us, the idea of feeling graceful and full of God's grace is not something that comes particularly easy. Practicing a little bit each day makes a world of difference.

Prayer

God, today I step into the winning circle. I step into the circle in which You have expected me to be standing all along. I stand in the place where I am loved; I love myself, and I easily love others. I stand tall, walk with ease and move with precision and grace. Those around me are amazed at Your light that shines through me. I am an example and inspiration to everyone I meet. I am a child of the most high God, and for that relationship, I am ever thankful. Amen.

Reflection: Cultivating Grace

Just how graceful do you feel on any given day? When was the last time you described yourself to someone (or yourself) as elegant and refined? What can you do to feel more graceful?

Activity: Find Your Signature Look

What we wear has a powerful impact on our mood. Today, spend some time in your closet. Maybe it needs a full overhaul or possibly just a bit of tidying up. After you have organized your space, pick out the outfit that makes you feel your best. Give it a special place in your closet. Make this your go-to look when you need a boost of confidence.

DAY 21:

DIALOGUE WITH GOD

"Then you will call on me and come and pray to me, and I will listen to you. You will seek me and find me when you seek me with all your heart." (Jeremiah 29:12, 13)

All sorts of cognitive issues come along with the autoimmunity experience. If waking in a veil of fog or struggling through a period of mental shutdown is something familiar, you might have also considered how to effectively pray during these times. Depression alone can cause challenges in our dialogue with God. Many people say the hardest part of working through mental confusion is taking the first steps toward trying to feel better. The nature of mental sluggishness tends to make us apathetic and unmotivated. The most important thing to remember is simply to start somewhere—even if that means reaching out to others for guidance and encouragement.

Prayer and solitude heal, but sometimes praying and being alone simply aren't enough. Mental confusion is one of those tricky areas where prayer alone is not enough. Like any other muscle in our body, if we want our mind to remain supple and useful, we have to push beyond the seeming limitations by challenging it with interesting and fun things. And sometimes when the mind is screaming to be left alone, we really need to push through to see the results we want. I am not talking about overdoing it when we don't feel well or being abusive; rather, I am addressing knowing healthy limits and working toward those. Don't feel like calling a friend but know it would be in your best interest? Then it is probably better to push through and make the phone call anyway. Maybe you aren't feeling like working on that project you have been putting off or you feel like you couldn't do your best at it now anyway. In some instances, simply starting the project can open up your mind to the ability to get it done. Remember, your daily actions are also a dialogue with God. The way you prepare your meals, interact with others and put your heart into your passions are an expression of love to our Creator.

Focus on consistency, not perfection. So many resources are available today to help us stay consistent with prayer. Prayer partners, online groups, and time-limited books like this one make it possible to stay connected to God—even when we really feel overwhelmed.

Prayer

Thank You for my ever-regenerating brain. It is an incredible time in which I live with the knowledge that my brain is not a fixed object but an ever-changing living organ that wants to learn and grow. The brilliance of Your physical creation amazes me daily. Every moment my brain seamlessly orchestrates to my body in order that I might think, move and breathe. The functions of my brain of which I am aware and those I do not fully understand are vast and endless. Today, I thank You for the gift of awareness and ask for increased clarity in all aspects of my life. Amen.

Reflection: Finding Clarity

How many times have you prayed to God for clarity? What was your experience? Are you actively doing things to keep your mind healthy? These things are even more important while you are healing!

Activity: Remembering What Works

What are some things that have helped untangle depression and mental confusion in the past? Write down these ideas and commit to revisiting them when you are feeling stuck.

WEEK 4:

UP FROM THE ASHES

This is our last week together. You have discovered a myriad of ways to enhance your prayer life and increase your ability to heal both physically and spiritually. So far we have focused on setting up conditions to heal and to pray, listening to our bodies more deeply, seeing painful experiences in various ways and finding new ways to support our healing. This week adds upon all the work you have already completed. Now, we'll focus on the ability to step into the world with conviction and confidence.

DAY 22

CONFIDENCE IN CHRIST

"For I am convinced that neither death nor life, neither angels nor demons, neither the present nor the future, nor any powers, neither height nor depth, nor anything else in all creation, will be able to separate us from the love of God that is in Christ Jesus our Lord."
(Romans 8:38, 39)

There are aspects of ourselves that we must closely guard during times of healing. Self-esteem is one of those tricky intangibles that can slip away from us amidst drastic physical changes, criticism from healthcare providers and family members, not to mention our own history of self- judgment and blame.

Some psychologists suggest that experiencing a chronic illness follows the same psychological adjustment of the stages of grief. First is the Crisis Phase. The shock of illness can be overwhelming, and all that we previously thought about our identity can be challenged. This time is spent in a frantic attempt to determine what is wrong as quickly as possible. Second, the Stabilization Phase is the period where you learn to restructure your life according to new limitations or abilities. Family members begin to accept new aspects of your life, including new financial and social roles. The Reconstruction Phase focuses on building new meaning in your life and a establishing a renewed sense of self. During this phase, your self-esteem and confidence go through a complete makeover! Whatever emotional challenges you faced during the earlier phases, you are starting to see some reconciliation and clarity. Lastly, the Integration Phase is the stage where you realize how much you have grown through the experience of illness and loss.

While these phases aren't linear, we can expect that we will not have to stay in a state of crisis forever. That said, we may have challenges making sense of our illness. Our entire life experience is about the stories we formulate for ourselves. The beauty is that we get to choose the story we want to live!

So choose a story that includes your understanding of Christ as the ultimate Role Model in self- esteem and confidence. Because Christ was human, He did have moments of confusion and He even doubted God's plan, asking why He was forsaken on the cross. However, in the end, Christ lived a life of incredible confidence. Remember: true confidence comes through Christ. Modeling the words and power of a man who could see our true nature, perform miracles and love unconditionally is the ultimate accomplishment for our lives.

Prayer

Christ, my Redeemer, support and unwavering Friend, all I ever have to do is look directly to You for help. You make it easy for me to plan my day, love my family and live a life of meaning. When I look in the mirror, I see a reflection of endless possibilities. Stepping out the door, I know that I can accomplish all things through You. Winding down in the evening, I can reflect on the achievements of the day. I know that I do all this through You who dwells in me. Amen.

Reflection: Assessing Confidence

What is an area of your life where you lack confidence? How can you look to Christ's life as an example of unlimited strength?

Activity: Scripture Meditation

Meditate on the following Scripture for 10 to 15 minutes and then write some personal experiences that arise from your meditation:

"For you have been my hope, Sovereign Lord,
my confidence since my youth.
6 From birth I have relied on you;
you brought me forth from my mother's womb.
I will ever praise you." (Psalm 71:5, 6)

DAY 23

CONNECTING TO TRUTH

"To the Jews who had believed him, Jesus said, 'If you hold to my teaching, you are really my disciples. 32 Then you will know the truth, and the truth will set you free." (John 8:31, 32)

One of the most influential writers on emotional and physical healing, Louise Hay, once lectured about the totality of possibilities. In this lecture, she reminded the audience of the vast universe in which we live where everything imaginable is happening in the present moment. In that lecture, she spoke of how we view our health from the perspective of limitless possibilities. Some of that lecture is as follows:

I live in the totality of possibilities. Where I am there is ALL good...In my health I go beyond age...I go beyond medical opinion...it isn't the truth of your being. It is medical opinion channeled through a particular person which is the popular belief of the day. I will not be limited by that. I go beyond incurable. Incurable only means they don't know how to cure it at the moment. It does not mean it is incurable.

Did you ever hear medical advice or opinion you simply knew wasn't accurate? Did someone tell you that you would never be able to enjoy the type of health you currently have? Endless accounts are available of people overcoming physical adversities no one ever thought possible. You are no different. Daily, our bodies are regenerating, growing and becoming new organisms—never to have existed before.

Learning to let go of opinions that do not serve your healing is a part of finding your truth. No other person can dictate your treatment or healing. Only you know the direction you need to take in making medical decisions. Accepting our physical experiences as they are and working to move in the direction of increased wellness are conscious choices we must make.

When we take the stance of supporting ourselves, we step into the truth that Jesus speaks of in John 8. Like Jesus, we might find ourselves completely misunderstood and in disagreement with those around us. As an example, Jesus reiterated He is the "I AM." When we follow Jesus' example and affirm clearly "I AM," we easily let go of the opinions of others. Knowing that through Christ's example, we live in the truth of our perfection, our healing easily comes.

Prayer

Heavenly Father, today I am committed to becoming honest with myself and with others about the areas of my life that need improvement. I look to Your earthly Son as an example of clarity of mind, right speech and action. Today I am committed to living this day to the fullest, correcting things that need to be corrected and acknowledging the areas of my life that are doing well. I pray this in Your Holy Name. Amen.

Reflection: Being Honest

Have there been issues in your life where you weren't honest with yourself? What impact, if any, has this lack of honesty had on your healing?

Activity: Making Amends

Are there any relationships in your life that you wish you had handled differently? If so, can you communicate more clearly or make improvements to the relationship now? If it isn't possible to communicate with the person you are thinking of, take some time to write out all the things you would say to them today.

DAY 24

LIGHTING UP THE ROOM

"You are the light of the world. A town built on a hill cannot be hidden.15 Neither do people light a lamp and put it under a bowl. Instead they put it on its stand, and it gives light to everyone in the house. 16 In the same way, let your light shine before others, that they may see your good deeds and glorify your Father in heaven."
(Matthew 5:14-16)

We are called to show the world our brilliance. We are all familiar with being part of an audience as it is common to go to movies, concerts and plays. But how many of us have had the opportunity to take the stage? If you have, you know the magical feeling of being able to portray parts of yourself through acting, music or dance. If you have never had the opportunity to physically be on a stage, you can still practice the feeling of being infinitely special and adored by those around you. Begin today to be the lead act in the deeply fascinating play of your life. Genesis 1:26 reminds us that we are made in God's image. Physically, we are the reflection of eternity. It doesn't get much more awe-inspiring than that realization! Like acting, our life is a reflection of whatever we choose to portray to the world.

The American actress, Marian Seldes, once said:

> *Confidence has nothing to do with what you look like. If you obsess over that, you'll end up being disappointed in yourself all the time. Instead, high self-esteem comes from how you feel in any moment. So walk into a room acting like you're in charge, and spend your energy on making the people around you happy.*

Marian's thought on social interactions is only one approach. As Christian women, we want the world to see us as loving, compassionate, confident reflections of our Divine Source. We show the world God's grace by sharing our gifts. Your gifts haven't stopped simply because you became ill. They haven't stopped because plans changed, and your life went in a different direction. Part of that really is the excitement of being alive, albeit hard to understand at times. In letting go of our expectations and accepting life for the moment-to-moment experience that it is, we can shine brightly in a world that desperately needs our light.

Prayer

Heavenly Father, you guide my every action. Today I step into my brilliance knowing that you guide me. I turn over my insecurities and allow for all the good things you have prepared for me. As I interact with others, I will remember the love that I intend to show the world through my actions. I ask that throughout the day I am reminded of the love I was born to reflect to the world. Amen.

Reflection: Recognizing Your Brilliance

When was a time you felt your most brilliant? Were you recognized for your accomplishments or was it a silent experience?

Activity: Go Play

Your activity today is to spend some time in play. The study of positive psychology is full of research validating how important play is for our confidence. Set aside time to play with your children, take a dance class, get involved in a group sport. Out of ideas? Begin a collage or vision board. Head on over to your local arts supply store to pick up a bunch of glitter, paper and markers! Whatever your idea of play, get to it today!

DAY 25

SINGING GOD'S PRAISE

"My mouth is filled with your praise, declaring your splendor all day long." (Psalm 71:8)

One of the most glorious things we have is our voice. Using our voice in praise is not about being a professional singer or being gifted with an incredible voice. Rather, it is using the voice we were given to the best of our ability. That means taking care in every way, including taking care of our physical body (throat, mouth and lungs), singing praises, and speaking with loving intention. Like our vision, something as simple as our voice can easily be taken for granted. In recognizing that our voice is a true gift, we can begin to cherish it and build up its potential for worship.

"In the beginning was the Word, and the Word was with God, and the Word was God." (John 1:1) It wasn't simply God's thoughts but His Words that spoke the entire universe into existence. This concept was explained in John to remind us that our words have the power to be life-changing. How we approach our healing begins with the words we use to describe it to others. Are we always speaking of illness? Do we mention our progress and moments of feeling healthy and strong? We can also begin to use our words to change the situations we find scary and difficult. We have enough difficult situations in our lives without using our words to make things worse. Make it a habit to stop negativity in discussions with others. Use your social time to share uplifting experiences and praise. The more you praise others (in an honest way), the more support you will receive.

Prayer

Heavenly Father I thank You for the connection of prayer. I thank you that I have language and the ability to express myself through my words. Today I acknowledge that my words have tremendous power to lift up others. I ask that my voice be an advocate for my needs and a support for those I come in contact with. This I ask in Your Name. Amen.

Reflection: Connecting Voice, Language, and Thoughts

Has your physical voice or speech pattern changed since diagnosis? What about your language? Has it become more difficult to convey thoughts? Have you become more negative/positive or has nothing changed?

Activity: Use Your Voice in a New Way

Today we revisit the voice.

Jot down some negative statements you say on a regular basis. Some examples might include apologizing for no reason, saying negative things about your situation or your body, or using phrases like "I hate..." Today, make it a point to recognize how often you say these types of statements. Try to incorporate more positive words in your vocabulary like "fabulous" and "joy."

DAY 26:

FINISHING WITH JOY

"For our light and momentary troubles are achieving for us an eternal glory that far outweighs them all. So we fix our eyes not on what is seen, but what is unseen, since what is seen is temporary, but what is unseen is eternal." (2 Corinthians 4:17, 18)

All of our life is a practice for dying. In other parts of the world and indigenous cultures, tremendous attention is given to the preparation and process of dying. Unlike these cultures, our modern lifestyle tends to view death as something to be ignored. Christ was the ultimate example of living in the present moment. He had no intention of ignoring any aspect of life, including his own physical death. In fact, He spent His entire life preparing for the experience of dying.

Because our culture does not provide many opportunities to explore the process of dying, we have to seek these out on our own. Our days are filled with so many opportunities to practice dying. Every inhale and exhale is a reminder of our ever-evolving bodies. Sleeping and waking allow us to practice being alive in the physical world and resting in peaceful stillness. Beginning and finishing projects, rearing children and caring for our parents are all wonderful opportunities to align ourselves with the process of endless change of which death is simply one aspect. Talking about death, rather than avoiding and denying it, makes it less scary and unknown.

So what does the Bible say about death? The Bible clearly describes physical death, a physical transition that does not take away from the eternal essence of who we are. Some verses to review include Revelations 21, Ecclesiastes 12, Romans 6, Luke 23:43 and John 11:26.

Death is simply another transition in God's eternal plan for your true essence. Now is the time to begin embracing and loving all aspects of our mortal life cycle, loving every season in which we find ourselves.

Prayer

Creator of everything that is born and passes away, I spend this day honoring all aspects of my life including the ending. I rejoice in the practicing of letting go. I let go of that which no longer serves me. I let go of the little things like my exhale. I let go of the big things like the idea that my physical form will last forever. Instead, I look clearly at the ebb and flow of life, loving every season that I experience. I praise You, and I am completely satisfied where I am.

Reflection: Looking At Death

How often do you think about your death? How did your family of origin experience and address dying?

Activity: Preparing for A Joyful Death

Today is a writing exercise around death and dying. Write your thoughts to the following statements/questions. Then, add your own thoughts on preparing for a joyful death.

What does the term "Joyful Death" mean to you?

What would be the ideal conditions under which you would die?

In what ways does acknowledging your mortality affect your daily life?

DAY 27:

WAKE UP TO GRACE

"And do this, understanding the present time: The hour has already come for you to wake up from your slumber, because our salvation is nearer now than when we first believed." (Romans 13:11)

In week two, we addressed the importance of taking care of our sleep cycle. Today, we take a look at waking up to our lives. The story of Christ's living, dying and being revived from the dead is the ultimate example of waking up to our lives. The idea that love above all things can save us from our circumstances and ourselves is the resounding message in the basis of Christianity. When we look at this in terms of healing our physical body and spirit, the focus becomes the ability to love more deeply than we ever have before.

All of us struggle with some level of self-sabotage and sticking points that we simply cannot seem to shake. Waking up means "letting go and making room for the ability for new life to come rushing in." Today, let's take the time to assess the matters and things that no longer serve us. Those things can be little or big. They can be things we care about or things that no longer have much meaning yet we have failed to get rid of them. From unnecessary spending to patterns of thinking that are harmful, what can you begin to let go of today in order to wake up to the life you deserve?

Waking up is the ultimate gift of being alive. As Christians, it is what we work toward every day. We can call it many different things—having a deeper connection with God, living a more Godly life, staying in the presence of God, living as Jesus lived. Whatever language you use, they are all the same goal: to accept the ultimate gift which is having a complete awareness of God in the present moment.

Prayer

Today, I affirmatively pray and clear my mind of all doubts and distractions. I accept God's presence in all aspects of my life, including my current ability to read and comprehend my actions, as well as my day-to-day tasks. I now receive the confidence and inspiration to move through life in the image of Christ who was fully awake, accepting of every aspect of being human. I know the living Spirit is flowing through me and freely shared toward all those whom I meet.

Reflection: Recalling the Memory of "Aliveness"

When was a time you felt most alive? What were the physical sensations that went along with that experience? Recall them now and try to feel them in this moment.

Activity: Music Therapy

Music is a powerful way to enjoy the present moment. Today spend time listening to your favorite song. Try listening as if you have never heard the song before. See if you can hear different aspects of the song you had never really noticed.

Additionally, there are many recordings that have been proven to reduce chronic pain. Recordings by David Ison are some of my favorite resources.

DAY 28:

RISE UP AND THRIVE

"And we know that in all things God works for the good of those who love him, who have been called according to his purpose." (Romans 8:28)

The science of thriving: i.e., "to grow and develop vigorously" has been researched increasingly over the past decade. In one research study by the Search Institute in Minneapolis, Minnesota, researchers studied the behaviors that distinguished between teenagers who thrived and those who were simply "getting by." They found that if teens focused on key ideas called "sparks" that they had a much greater likelihood of thriving as adults. Sparks are "the activities in which you engage that make you feel your very best." Sparks include anything you enjoy from music to your career to being with your family.

Have there been times in your life when you felt that you were simply "getting by"? Being enthusiastic about life does not simply happen on its own. We absolutely must seek out ways to feel excited about our circumstances. But practicing being excited is somewhat harder than it sounds. Today is the day to begin turning off the negative thoughts that stop us from living our best life.

Some Steps to Thriving:

Step One: Observe your circumstances as perfect and whole. The time to stop thinking "Life will be better when..." is right now. God created the present moment for you to experience fully, without question or complaint.

Step Two: Anticipate that things will work out for you. Living in expectancy and excitement is the basis of being successful in everything we do.

Step Three: Rise up and thrive today. Start to find small ways to feel accomplished and successful right now.

Prayer

I am grateful for success in all things. I continue to grow into better and better versions of myself, remembering the God presence in everything I do. Today, I let nothing enter my consciousness that will distract me from rising up and thriving. I am completely protected and know that good attends me always. Because I stand in the knowledge that I am perfect and whole, I can move forward with ease.

Reflection: Reflecting on Accomplishments

What has been your greatest accomplishment? What is your greatest dream? What have you done today to take steps toward accomplishing those things?

Activity: What Is Your Spark?

Make a list of what excites and makes you the happiest. Then answer the following questions:

When was the last time you participated in your spark?

What excuses have you used to stop participating in your spark?

Are there any ways you can start spending a bit more time doing your spark?

DAY 29:

I AM AMAZING AND AMAZED

"I praise you because I am fearfully and wonderfully made. Your works are wonderful, I know that full well."
(Psalm 139:14)

Have you ever been so caught up in an activity that you lost track of time? This experience has been coined by positive psychologists as being in "flow." "The ability to stop being self-conscious while participating in something" is the liberating feeling common to athletes and musicians. Being in flow is often referred to as being "in the zone." This incredibly pleasant place for the brain is another way to nourish ourselves on a daily basis. Much like in meditation, this flow state can lead to dramatically improved enjoyment and quality of life. Today, we focus on how to incorporate "finding flow" into our prayer practice.

The premier researcher on the subject of flow is Mihaly Csikszentmihalyi. In 1975 he noted six factors that make up a flow experience:

- Intense and focused concentration on the present moment
- Merging of actions and awareness
- A loss of reflective self-consciousness
- A sense of control over the situation

- A distortion of temporal experience (lose track of time)
- Experience of the activity as rewarding

Have your prayer experiences ever had elements of the flow factors listed in the previous paragraph? Have you ever ended a prayer session with an overall physical feeling of euphoria, extreme happiness or bliss? If so, then you already experienced the benefits of flow as a part of your prayer experience. Think back to that time and try to remember what might have caused such a wonderful feeling. Were you praying aloud in a group? Maybe you weren't even praying at all but engaged in praise worship, singing or dancing. Fantastic! Whatever your reference, the idea is that your prayer life is absolutely not limited to sitting alone with eyes closed, dialoguing with God. In fact, active prayer can be some of the most powerful, transformative prayer experiences we have.

Prayer

God of everything, I can comprehend I am amazing and pray with gratitude, knowing all things are provided in every moment. My physical body, emotions, spiritual life and connections to others are included in Your creation. Through prayer I turn all relationships and experiences deemed difficult into

opportunities to become more fully alive.
Reflection: Recalling Feelings of "Awe"

When was the last time something took your breath away? What are ways that you can experience this feeling more often?

Activity: Turn It Into a Prayer!

Today choose an activity you have to do. Then pick a simple prayer phrase (meditators call it a mantra), and try to repeat this phrase throughout your task. Try silently repeating your prayer phrase while taking a walk, washing dishes or running errands. You can also reword your phrase to match the activity you are doing. For example while cleaning, use statements like "I walk with grace" or "I am made new."

Sample prayer phrases or words:

- I Am That I Am!

- God Is Love!

- Joy

- Amazing Grace!

- I Surrender All

- Love Is Here

DAY 30:

THE UNLIMITED EXPERIENCE OF GOD

"In the same way, let your light shine before others, that they may see your good deeds and glorify your Father in heaven." (Matthew 5:16)

Exploring your relationship with God through prayer is an ever-evolving process. Life is always going to come up with new ways for us to experience glimpses of divinity and wholeness. It is up to us to seek these new ways of understanding. Fresh experiences are not reserved for children; they are available to us in every moment. The two categories of experiencing we have covered this month have been through prayer and our physical experience. But there is one more—our connection with those around us.

Body awareness is a term used in dance and physical education to describe how people understand what is happening in their body as well as how they are moving through space. Some people are naturally better at this than others, and, fortunately, it is also something that can be learned and improved upon. The more we practice a sport, learn a martial art or any other physical skill, we are becoming more familiar with how our body works. The same is true with experiencing an illness. The process of healing and recovery is an excellent time to practice listening to the subtle and not-so-subtle cues of our body's inner workings. The more we practice listening to our body in activity and stillness, the more enjoyable is our experience within it.

The opportunity to grow spiritually by using our physical experience, while sometimes painful, can also be a source of inspiration and connection with those around us. You have an incredible story that is both unique and so relatable right now. One way to know that your healing is going in the right direction is when you are ready to begin connecting with the eternal part of those around you. People want to hear about your struggle and your accomplishments. They also want to know that they can heal, that life can be rich, full, and happy, despite what some would consider a negative event.

Prayer

My life is a gift to those around me. My experiences are a platform of hope and connection. Today, I recognize that essentially we are all the same. We all want improvement and healing in our lives. We all seek renewal and acceptance. I acknowledge my uniqueness and appreciate the opportunity to use my life to connect with others. My story is valuable. My experience makes me unique and connects me with people that will benefit from it. I thank you for this life. Amen

Reflection: Exploring Gifts and Talents

What gifts and talents do you easily share with others? Are there other ones you could also share? How have difficulties in your life impacted your ability to connect? What can you do to make connection easier?

Activity: Share a Bit of Your Healing

Today, find some way to connect with others through your story. Find an online group or call someone in your church community to share your experience. If you are ready to share in a group, ask your minister if you can speak to your congregation about your healing experience.

Closing

This 30 Days of Prayer is a small stepping stone in your healing. I hope that this past month has brought a deeper awareness of the resources already available to you.

As you've lived, prayed and traveled along this 30 day journey, I hope that you have found comfort in knowing that you walk this path with many who share your experience with autoimmunity and that God walks it with us. I hope that you remember to acknowledge His presence and draw on His strength so that you, too, may live more fully in prayer as well as more in the moment.

Endnotes

Day 1 Anonymous. (2011). Still Small Voice 10: Creating A Prayer Space-Some Tips. Retrieved from http://www.movement.org.uk/blog/still-small-voice-10-creating-prayer-space-some-tips

Day 6 Carlson, Larissa Hall, RYT. (2012). Body Scan Meditation For Relaxation http://kripalu.org/blog/thrive/2012/12/13/body-scan-meditation-for-relaxation/

Day 7 Cuddy, Amy. (2012). Your Body Language Shapes Who You Are. TED Global 2012. Retrieved from http://www.ted.com/talks/amy_cuddy_your_body_language_shapes_who_you_are?language=en

Day 10 Ray, Linda. (2013). Box Breathing. Livestrong.com. Retrieved from http://www.livestrong.com/article/74944-box-breathing-technique/

Day 11 Pardi, Dan. (2013). The Myers Way Episode 10: Sleep Expert Dan Pardi. amymyersmd.com

Retrieved from
http://www.amymyersmd.com/2013/06/tmw-episode-10-sleep-expert-dan-pardi/

Day 12 Block PhD, Andrew. (2007). 11 Pain Control Techniques. Spinehealth.com Retrieved from
http://www.spine-health.com/conditions/chronic-pain/11-chronic-pain-control-techniques

Day 15 Wahls, Terry MD. (2014). Minding Your Mitochondria. TEDx Iowa City. Retrieved from
http://terrywahls.com/minding-your-mitochondria-dr-terry-wahls-at-tedxiowacity/

Day 16 Rubin, Michael MDCM. (2014). Overview of the Cranial Nerves. merckmanuals.com Retrieved from
http://www.merckmanuals.com/home/brain_spinal_cord_and_nerve_disorders/cranial_nerve_disorders/overview_of_the_cranial_nerves.html

Day 18 Rinpoche, Trungram Gyaltrul. (2015). Practices: Stillness Meditation. Dharmakaya.org Retrieved from
http://dharmakaya.org/practices/stillness-meditation/

Day 19 Berceli, David, PhD. (2015). Tension, Stress & Trauma Release Exercises. traumaprevention.com Retrieved from http://traumaprevention.com/what-is-tre/

Day 22 Kubler Ross, Elizabeth. (2014). On Death and Dying. Scribner

Day 23 Hay, Louise. (2005). The Totality of Possibilities Audio CD. HayHouse

Day 27 Ison, David. (2010). The Ison Method. theisonmethod.com Retrieved from http://www.theisonmethod.com/Pain-management-Programs.html

Day 28 Search Insitute. (2015). Sparks and Thriving. search-institute.org Retrieved from search-institute.org/sparks

Day 29 Csikszentmihaly, Mihaly. (1975). Beyond Boredom and Anxiety. London: Jossey-Bass Publishers

About The Author

RUSCHELLE KHANNA, LCSW is a psychotherapist and health advocate who speaks on topics of chronic disease. A dancer, meditator, and lover of all things travel, she is a graduate of Columbia University and has advanced training in Rational Emotive Behavioral Therapy and hypnotherapy. Ruschelle has helped thousands of men and women regain their lives over her decade of experience as a leader and practitioner in nonprofit management.

Ruschelle is also an advocate for functional medicine as a foundational way to address physical and mental illness. Through her healing journey from Neurological Lyme Disease, she has learned to utilize the experience of physical pain as a catalyst for present moment living. In teaching contemplative prayer, mindfulness and cognitive-behavioral strategies, she leads individuals and groups to experience new ways of healing.

She currently resides in Manhattan with her husband, dog and one grumpy cat.

You can reach her at

http://www.30daysofprayer.org

23051690R00068